MY STIGMATA

SAINT PADRE PIO SPEAKS

BOOK 3

GARGANO - SEP 15: Interior of Santuario
Santa Maria delle Grazie in San Giovanni
Rotondo, Italy. September 15, 2013

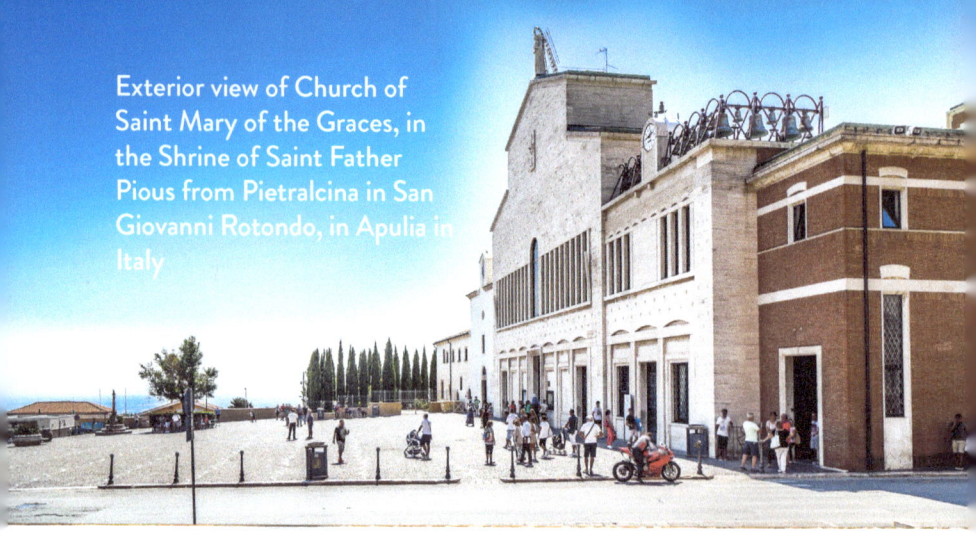

Exterior view of Church of Saint Mary of the Graces, in the Shrine of Saint Father Pious from Pietralcina in San Giovanni Rotondo, in Apulia in Italy

Saint Padre Pio Speaks - Book 3: My Stigmata

Published by Abba Books LLC
abbabooksllc@gmail.com
Copyright © 2025 Marie-Josée Thibault

All Rights Reserved

No part of this publication may be reproduced, distributed, or transmitted in any form or by any means, including photocopying, recording, or other electronic or mechanical methods, without the prior written permission of the publisher.

First Edition, 2025
Designed and Edited by Abba Books LLC
ISBN: 978-1-967429-01-1

Abba Books LLC
34972 Newark Blvd, #441
Newark, CA 94560

www.abbamyfatheriloveyou.com
https://www.facebook.com/AbbaILoveYouBooks/

Thy Peace on Earth must be achieved. No light, no litany must be spared to honor Thy Grace.
-Saint Paul

Content

Preface	VI
Chapter 1	1
Chapter 2	3
Chapter 3	5
Chapter 4	7
Chapter 5	9
Chapter 6	11
Chapter 7	13
Chapter 8	15
Chapter 9	17
Chapter 10	19
Chapter 11	21
Chapter 12	23
Chapter 13	25
Chapter 14	27
Chapter 15	29
Chapter 16	31
Chapter 17	33

Chapter 18	35	Chapter 27	53
Chapter 19	37	Chapter 28	55
Chapter 20	39	Chapter 29	57
Chapter 21	41	Chapter 30	59
Chapter 22	43	Chapter 31	61
Chapter 23	45	Chapter 32	63
Chapter 24	47	Chapter 33	65
Chapter a25	49		
Chapter 26	51		

My friends, my loves, my hearts, listen to me well,

Saint Padre Pio is a very important Saint in Heaven just as he is on Earth. His stigmata are wide open for all those who are in love with God. Padre Pio and my Son and are forever fused—for they are my joy and the Father's greatest joy. The glory of Abba Father continues to be made great through the stigmata of Saint Padre Pio and Saint Francis. I love you.

The Virgin Mary, Your Divine Mother

San Giovanni Rotondo, Italy

Preface

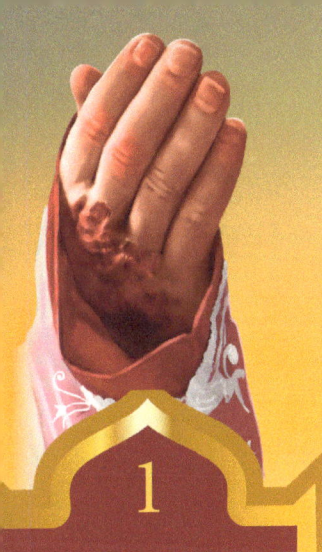

y children in distress, my loves, listen to me carefully.

The aim of this presentation is to explain to you in detail my stigmata, as well as those of my father, Father Francis of Assisi, whom I honor here in this book blessed by God.

Alleluia! Alleluia! Alleluia! Blessed are those who read this book today, for today, the Mercy contained in the stigmata is revealed. Amen! Alleluia!

I Love You, Pio

I Love You, Pio

2

My children of Sacred Love, listen to me carefully. Nothing can warn you of the danger you face as you walk this lost and decaying land except the Mercy contained within the stigmata. Know, dear children of my heart, that the Force of Redemption contained within the stigmata is stronger than the enemy, larger than all of creation, and more magnificent than the roses impregnated with dew in the morning.

Alleluia! Alleluia! Alleluia! Blessed are those invited to read this book, which is filled with transcendence, science, art, and, above all, Love.

I love you.

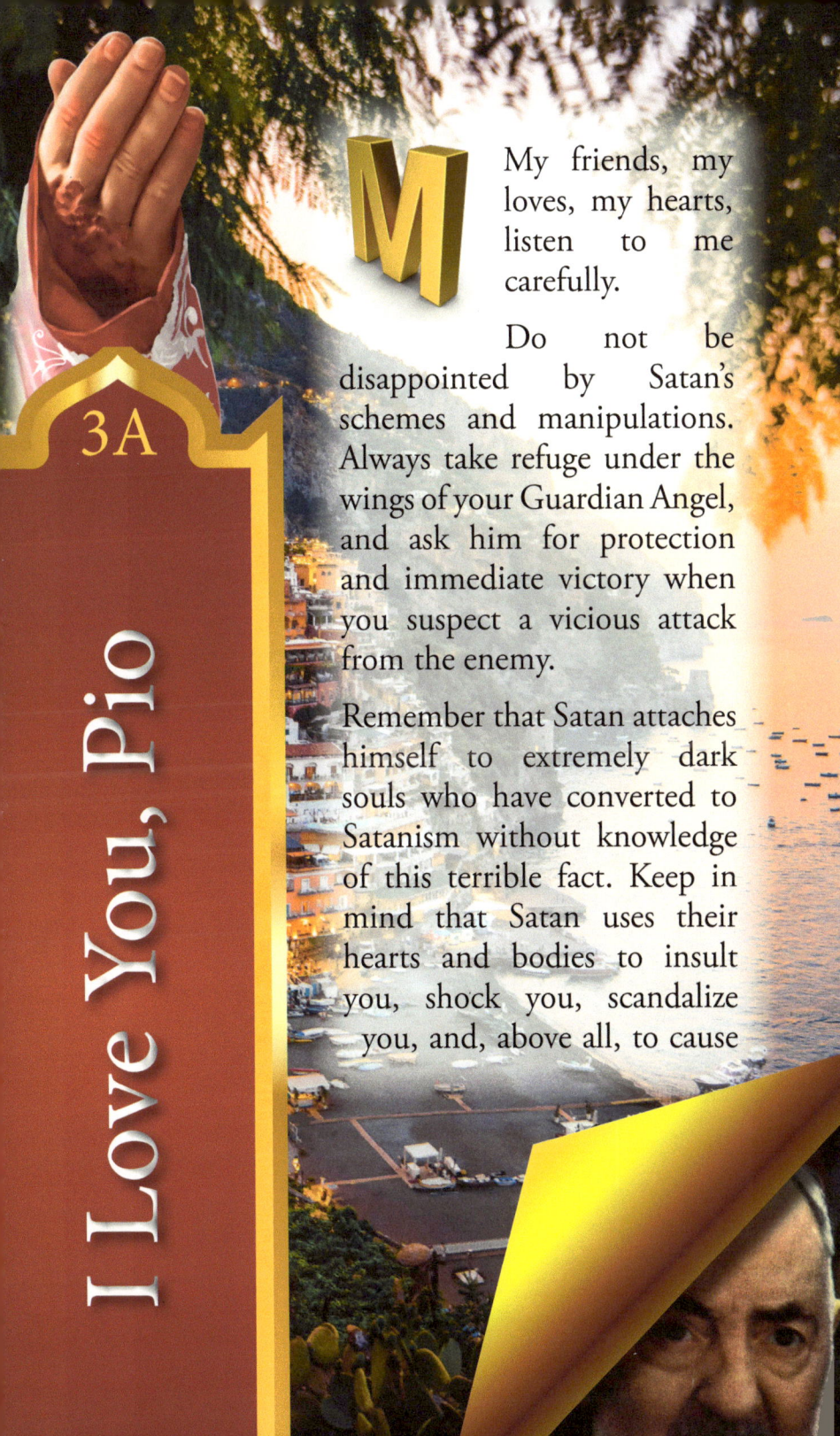

I Love You, Pio — 3A

My friends, my loves, my hearts, listen to me carefully.

Do not be disappointed by Satan's schemes and manipulations. Always take refuge under the wings of your Guardian Angel, and ask him for protection and immediate victory when you suspect a vicious attack from the enemy.

Remember that Satan attaches himself to extremely dark souls who have converted to Satanism without knowledge of this terrible fact. Keep in mind that Satan uses their hearts and bodies to insult you, shock you, scandalize you, and, above all, to cause

you to fall and sin before the Throne of God, the Father Almighty.

Alleluia! Alleluia! Alleluia! Blessed are those who detect Satan and his schemes by identifying the extreme behavior of people around them. Those who effectively fight Satan with the help of the Angels are also blessed. Amen! Alleluia!

3B

I Love You, Pio

I Love You, Pio

4

My souls in my holy hands, listen to me carefully.

I love you more than words can express. My stigmata—vessels of unique and incomparable redemption—transport me into a dimension of ineffable love for all humanity. I cannot contain my joy when you read these words, because I am in front of you, dear child in distress, at this very moment as you read these lines. I love you.

Alleluia! Alleluia! Alleluia! Blessed are the readers of this ineffable book, gift of God the Father, who is Pure and Original Love. Amen!

I Love You, Pio

My loves of Love, listen to me carefully.

Today, you will learn about the powers contained in my stigmata. My stigmata, my loves, represent the Mercy of God not just in its most visible, physical manifestation, but its most transcendent and most eloquent.

By this, I mean that my stigmata are symbols, powers, miracles, and, above all, Love embodied in my flesh. I love you.

Alleluia! Alleluia! Alleluia! Blessed are those who open their hearts to the palpable and transcendent Divine Mercy contained within my stigmata. Amen! Alleluia!

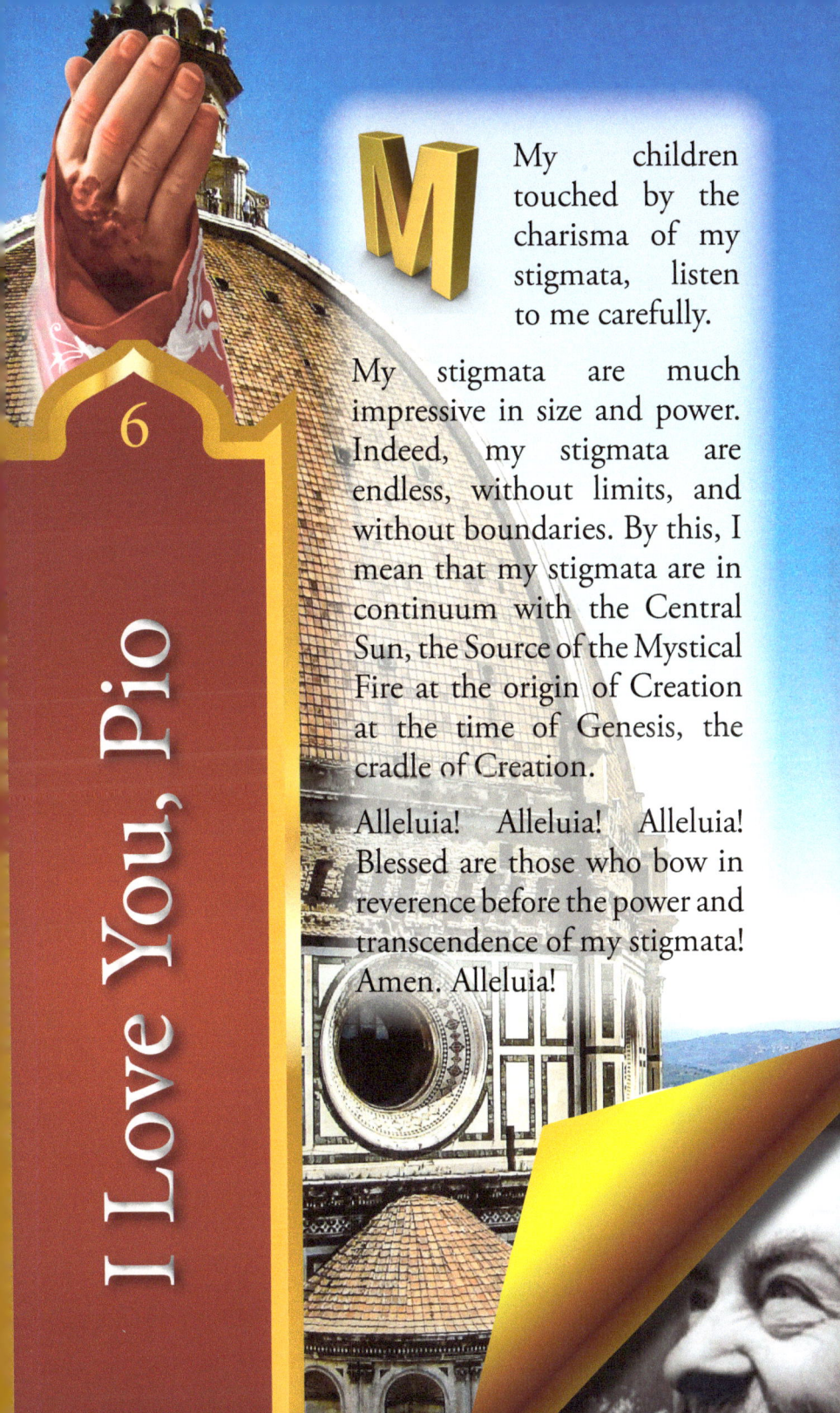

I Love You, Pio — 6

My children touched by the charisma of my stigmata, listen to me carefully.

My stigmata are much impressive in size and power. Indeed, my stigmata are endless, without limits, and without boundaries. By this, I mean that my stigmata are in continuum with the Central Sun, the Source of the Mystical Fire at the origin of Creation at the time of Genesis, the cradle of Creation.

Alleluia! Alleluia! Alleluia! Blessed are those who bow in reverence before the power and transcendence of my stigmata! Amen. Alleluia!

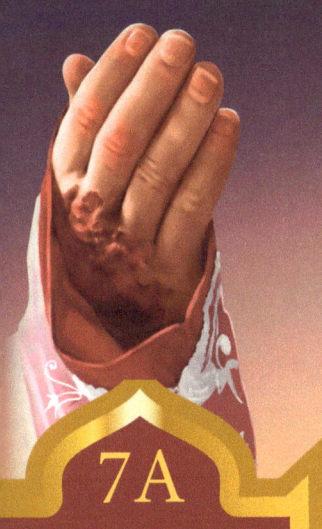

7A

I Love You, Pio

My children of the whole Earth, listen to me carefully.

Today, I want to draw your attention, your awareness, and your awakening to my stigmata. I talk not just about my stigmata, but also those of my father, Saint Francis of Assisi.

Do the following exercise: Look at any effigy made in my image, greet me, love me, and ask me to transport you to Heaven and ensure that your soul takes its place at my side—in front of me and in my heart.

You will feel your body become light, drowsy, at peace, and, above all, in love with the

Father, Jesus and Mary.

Alleluia! Alleluia! Alleluia! Blessed are those who love my stigmata, for God the Father will reward them. Amen! Alleluia!

7B

I Love You, Pio

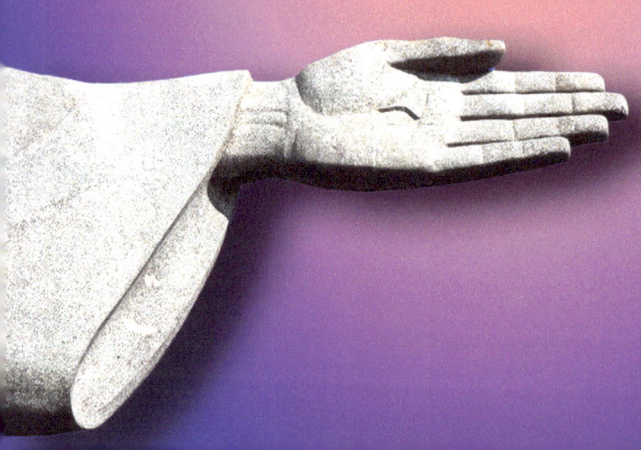

I Love You, Pio

8A

My friends of Love, listen to me and stay blessed. My stigmata are wide open to you, dear readers of this book blessed by God. By this, I mean that a divine and powerful Mercy has been bestowed upon you here, now, at the moment in which you read these lines.

This Grace is unique among all the Graces that God grants to humanity. Be generous and enter into a state of deep and sincere gratitude before God, who grants you this Grace at this blessed moment.

Alleluia! Alleluia! Alleluia! Blessed are those to whom my stigmata are wide open,

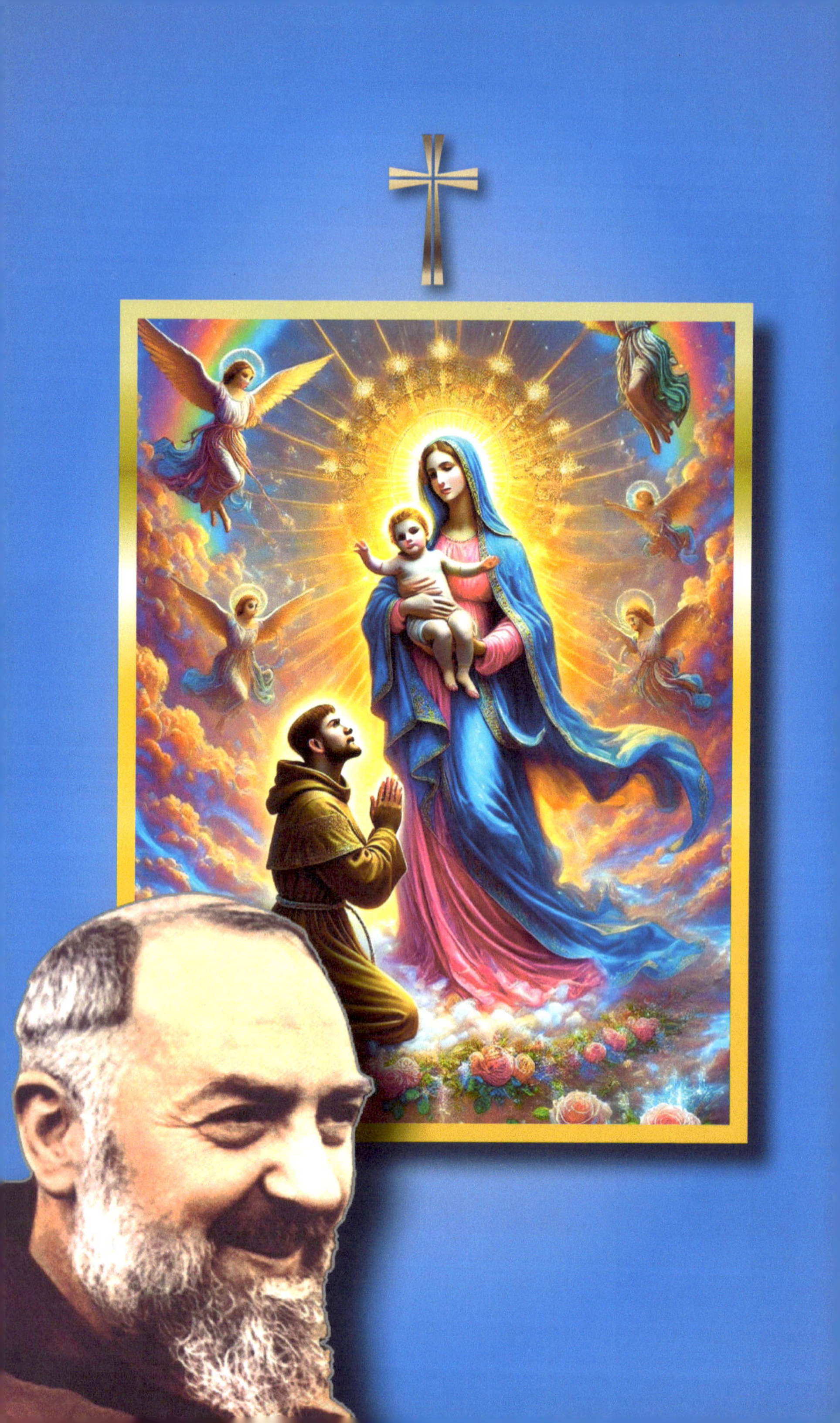

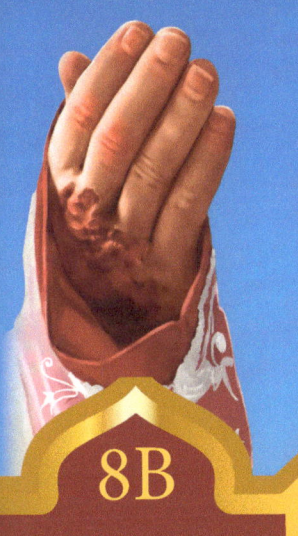

as the Mercy found therein is of a miraculous order with no limit.

I love you.

Amen! Alleluia!

8B

I Love You, Pio

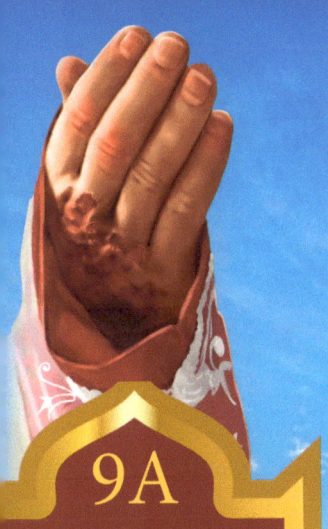

9A

I Love You, Pio

My friends, my loves, my hearts, listen to me carefully. Your soul, which is before my eyes as you read these lines at this very moment, is clothed with a unique, heavenly glory due to my holy influence and my blessing, which has manifested since you began reading this God-blessed book.

Do not forget, dear children of Love, that the love I have for you is transcendent, luminous, cosmic, eternal, and, above all, Christlike. My fusion with Christ, manifested by my stigmata, allows me to love you on a cosmic scale that you cannot understand. Only

at the time of the Great Day of Judgment will you learn of my holy influence and how I have benefited your life, which has been distinguished by my honorable presence.

Alleluia! Alleluia! Alleluia! Blessed are those who pray, love, and rejoice in Christ and the Virgin Mary. Blessed as well are those who have my name on their lips, for the Graces of Heaven are offered to them. Amen! Alleluia! I love you.

I Love You, Pio

9B

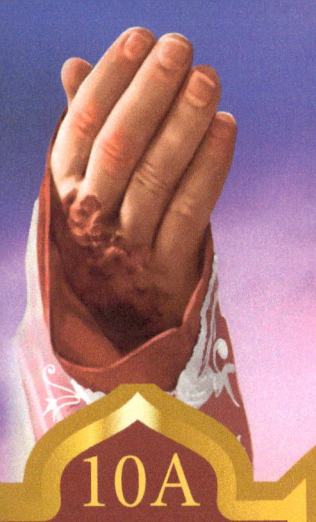

I Love You, Pio

10A

My children, I speak to you seriously.

Come, my children; come into my arms on this day of Grace! For the cosmic ray, which is my holy presence in your life, is amplified every day—progressively, and systematically—regardless of the regularity and piety of your prayers.

For I am with you at any time of the day and night.

Our union is real, eternal, spiritual, and, above all, bathed in the Light and Love of Christ Jesus, our Savior who loves you so much. I love you.

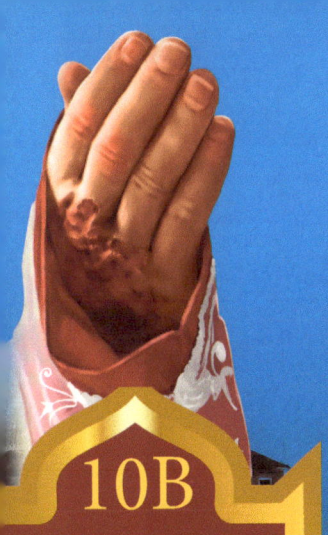

Alleluia! Alleluia! Alleluia! Blessed are those who are united to me for eternity— one day, we will walk together in the miraculous paths of Paradise, and the beatitudes therein will delight you limitlessly.

Amen! Alleluia!

10B

I Love You, Pio

11A

I Love You, Pio

My children of divine Grace, listen to me carefully.

No matter your belief in me and Father Saint Francis of Assisi, I stand beside you. The bond that unites us is obligatory and, above all, desired on my part in the sense that I am linked to you for eternity thanks to your reading of this book, regardless of whether you truly believe in these words and in this gigantic and fantastic promise.

Such is the power of these books and this collection discussing Saints from Paradise who speak to humanity, in addition to the words of Abba

Father and the Angels of God.

Grace be given to Marie-Josée, the author of these blessed books and the individual taking down this dictation at this moment.

Alleluia! Alleluia! Alleluia! Blessed are those invited to join me here and in the promised Paradise, for they are chosen here and now thanks to this book, which is blessed by God.

Amen! Alleluia!

I Love You, Pio

11B

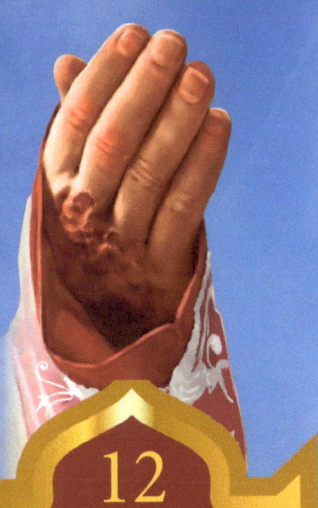

M My children in my arms, I look at you lovingly.

The blood that flows from my stigmata is type O negative—the universal donor. This is because this blood is that of Jesus Christ.

I will explain this cosmic and supernatural phenomenon to you in the following chapters.

Alleluia! Alleluia! Alleluia! Blessed are those who are touched by my blood, for Grace incarnate, Jesus Himself, our King and our God, truly touches them. Amen! Alleluia! I love you.

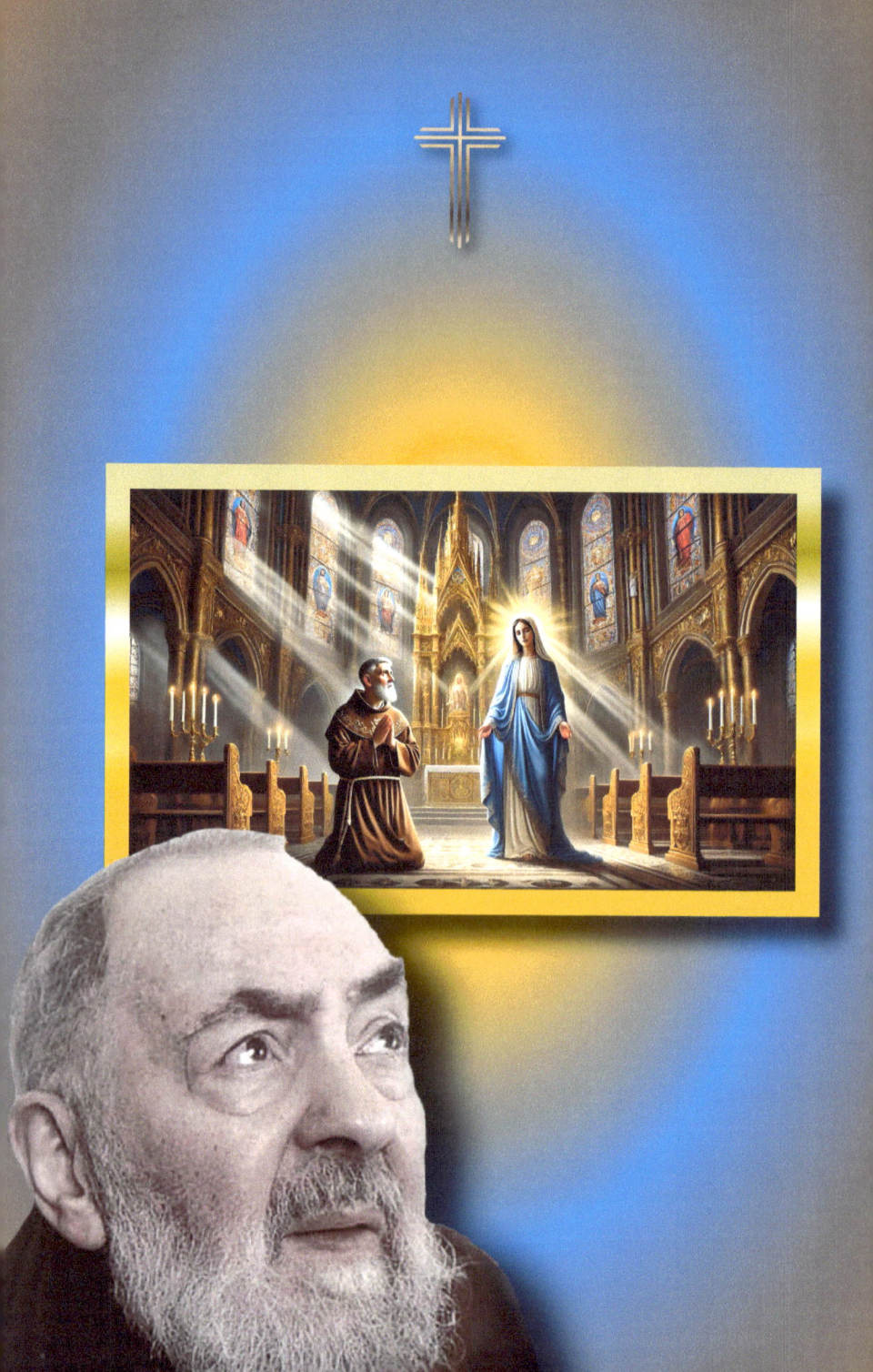

I Love You, Pio

13A

MHearts of my heart, listen to me carefully.

I do not know how to express, from the depths of my heart and my holy soul, the profound meaning of our union established here at this moment as you read these lines. Several other books have been offered to you on planet Earth that mention my name as well as my attributed prayers, conversations, instructions, and especially affirmations.

These books are written by generally honest and dedicated authors; however, rest assured that my voice and my regular visitations are exclusively directed to Marie-Josée, the

essence of Saint Paul on Earth, who takes this dictation before me here and now and is Abba Father's vessel of Grace.

Alleluia! Alleluia! Alleluia! Blessed are those who pray with me, bond with me, share love and hope with me, and above all, are absorbed in my stigmata for the greater glory of God the Father Almighty. Amen! Alleluia!

13B

I Love You, Pio

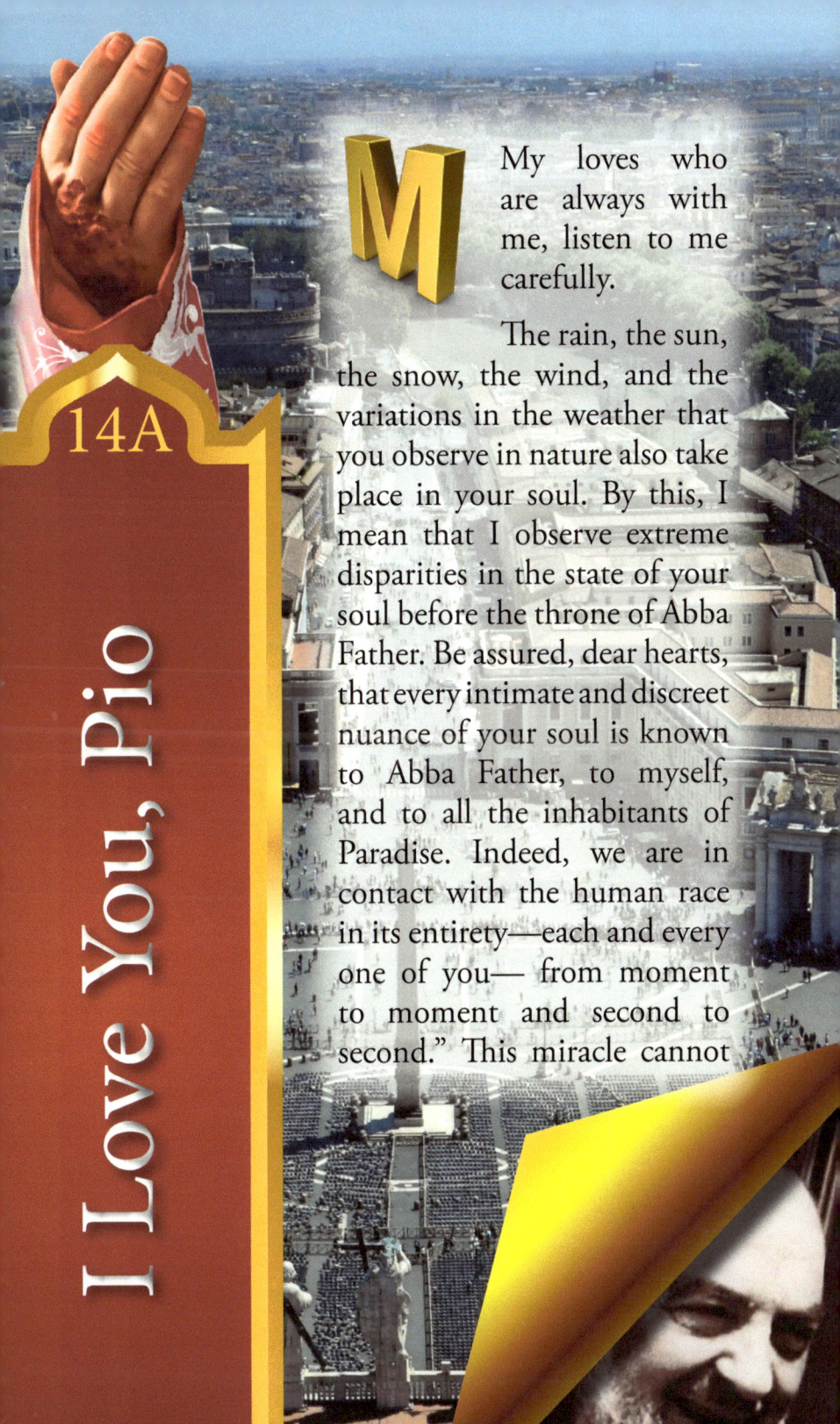

14A

I Love You, Pio

My loves who are always with me, listen to me carefully.

The rain, the sun, the snow, the wind, and the variations in the weather that you observe in nature also take place in your soul. By this, I mean that I observe extreme disparities in the state of your soul before the throne of Abba Father. Be assured, dear hearts, that every intimate and discreet nuance of your soul is known to Abba Father, to myself, and to all the inhabitants of Paradise. Indeed, we are in contact with the human race in its entirety—each and every one of you— from moment to moment and second to second." This miracle cannot

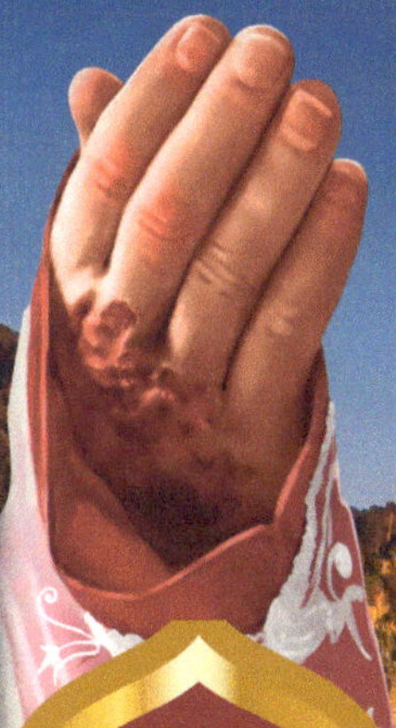

14B

I Love You, Pio

be understood by the human intellect.

Alleluia! Alleluia! Alleluia! Blessed are those who walk on this Earth knowing that they are protected, guided, inspired, but above all loved by the Saints of Paradise, the Angels of God, as well as by all the inhabitants of Paradise. Amen! Alleluia! I love you.

15A

I Love You, Pio

My loves, my hearts, listen to me carefully.

It is of critical and momentous interest today that you understand the profound mystery of stigmata.

The stigmata, my beloved, are vessels of Grace from the Abba Father. Imagine tunnels of intense light that originate in your heavy and black dimension and that end and lead directly to Paradise. When I absorb you into my stigmata, your soul is projected with prodigious speed through a tunnel of Glory, of Mercy, of Light, and, above all, of Love. I will now explain to you the meaning of the blood of Jesus.

I love you.

Alleluia! Alleluia! Alleluia! Blessed are the souls who are absorbed in my stigmata, as their center of gravity is immediately transported to the Paradise promised to them. Amen! Alleluia!

I Love You, Pio

15B

I Love You, Pio — 16A

My Hearts of love and glory, listen to me carefully.

I am happy only when my stigmata are active and absorbing the souls chosen by God for the Divine Mercy enclosed in these stigmata. The blood of Jesus, in its profound and transcendent essence, constitutes the divine cosmic Grace necessary for the accomplishment of this beautiful miracle of redemption.

The blood of Jesus is the blood of God, and this blood is the way, the truth, and the life — it is necessary for the salvation of your soul through the resurrection of our Beloved

16B

I Love You, Pio

Savior. I love you.

Alleluia! Alleluia! Alleluia! Blessed are those invited to cross the tunnel of my stigmata—a tunnel made possible thanks to the blood shed by Jesus our Savior and our Lord. Amen! Alleluia!

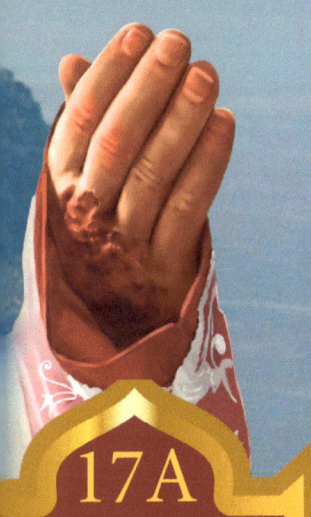

17A

I Love You, Pio

My friends, my loves, listen to me carefully.

Never in the history of humanity has there been so much Mercy on Earth, except for the time of the holy and immaculate life of Jesus Christ our Savior on Earth more than 2000 years ago.

Indeed, the Mercy granted to you through my holy stigmata is unique in its truth, power, eternal duration, and, above all, Love.

Through this Mercy I desire to instill in you a new motivation, a redoubled hope, a multiplied fervor in prayers, and, above all, a truer and more emotional love towards

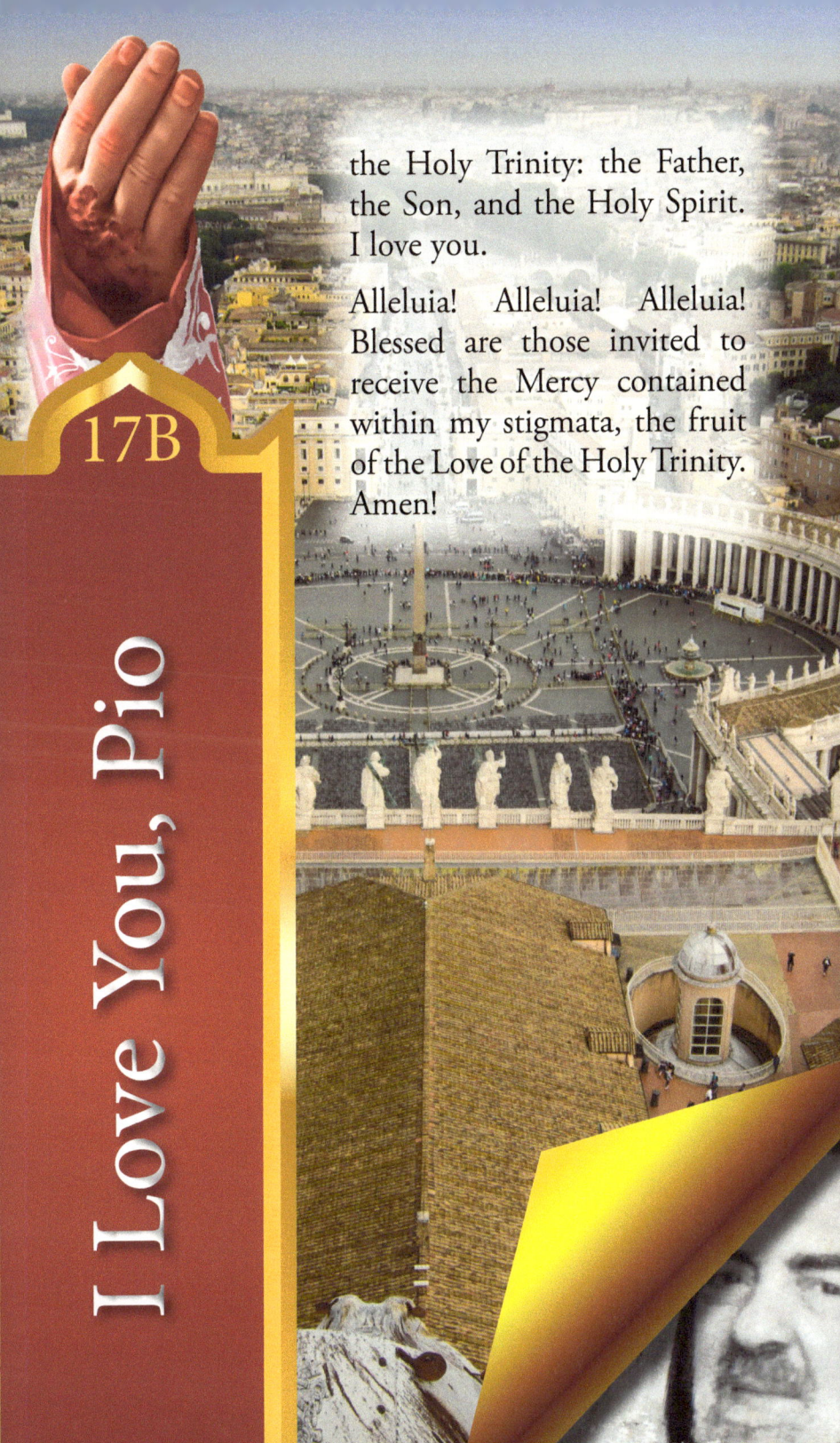

17B — I Love You, Pio

the Holy Trinity: the Father, the Son, and the Holy Spirit. I love you.

Alleluia! Alleluia! Alleluia! Blessed are those invited to receive the Mercy contained within my stigmata, the fruit of the Love of the Holy Trinity. Amen!

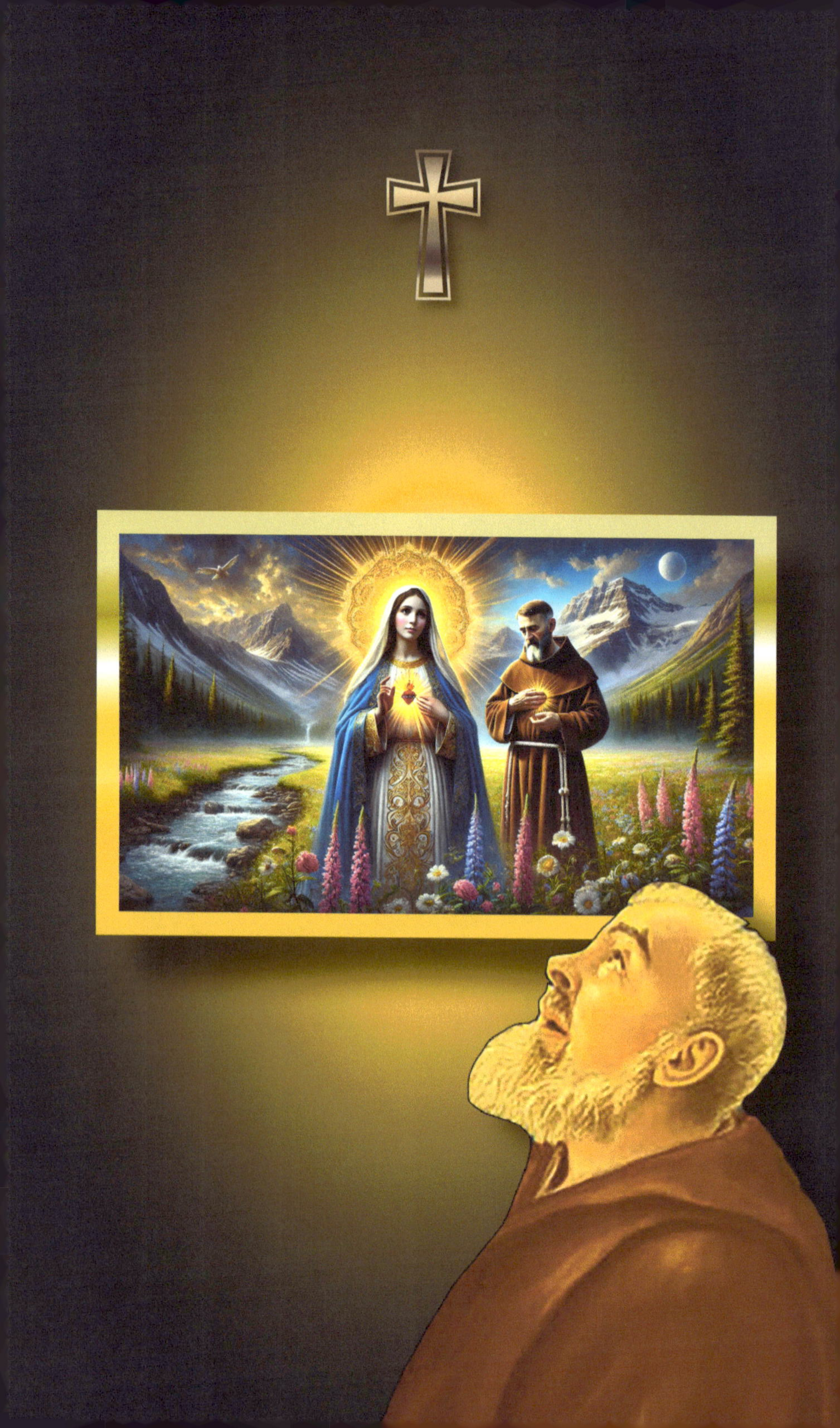

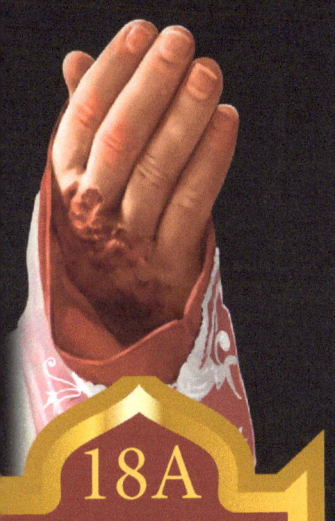

18A — I Love You, Pio

MDear hearts of glory, listen to me carefully.

Father Francis of Assisi and I are constantly collaborating and discussing the personal and unique situations of each and every one of you, no matter how numerous you are.

Indeed, Father Francis and I are united in higher and ineffable dimensions in which time and distance have no limitations in relation to the powers of Mercy contained in our stigmata. I will explain to you soon the transcendent meaning of our stigmata, which are in fact in cosmic and eternal union. I love you.

Alleluia! Alleluia! Alleluia!

Blessed are those invited to experience the Divine Mercy enclosed within the stigmata of Father Francis as well as my stigmata, for Father Francis and I are servants of God in a high-order, mystical union of prayer. Amen!

Alleluia!

18B

I Love You, Pio

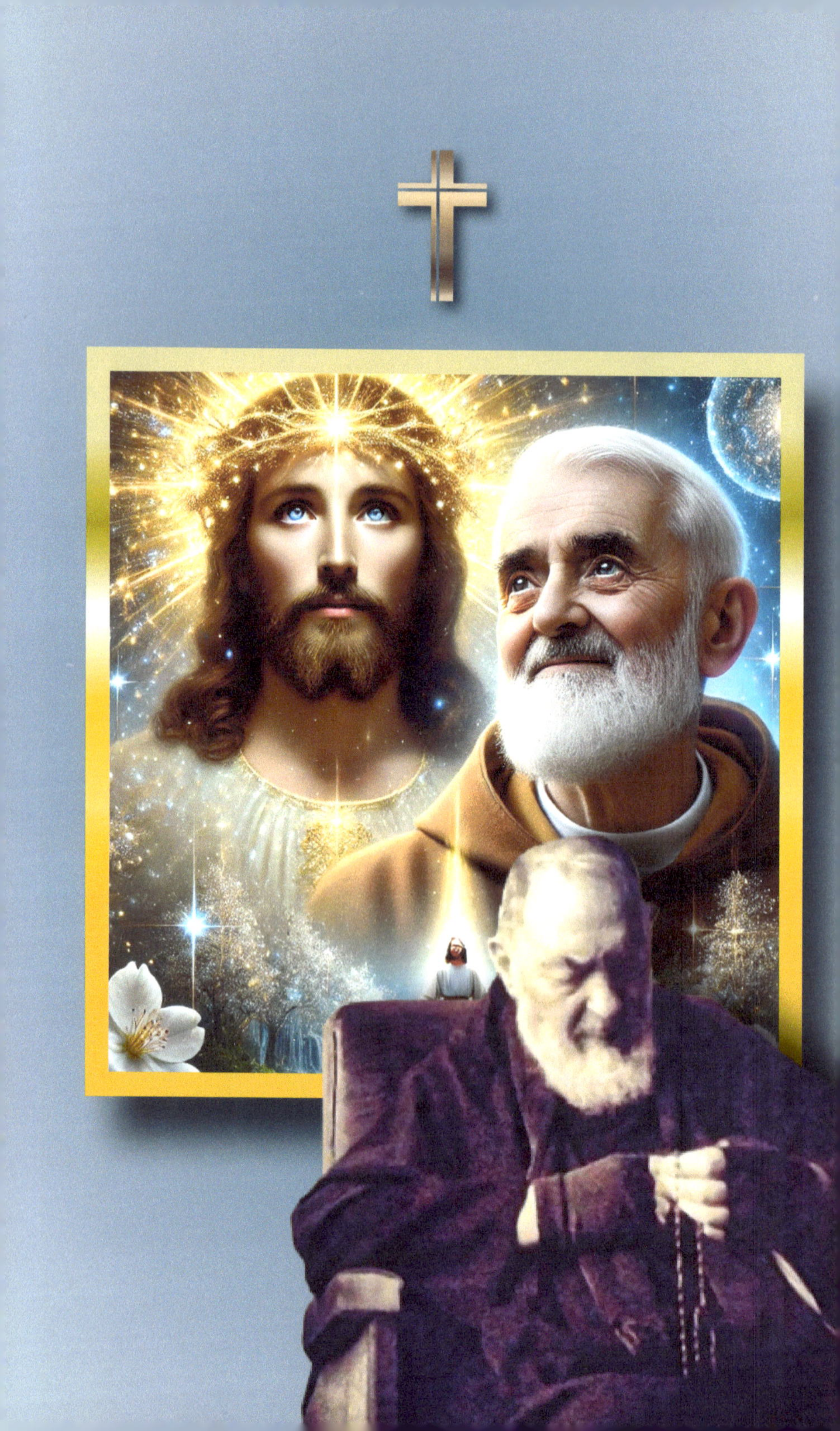

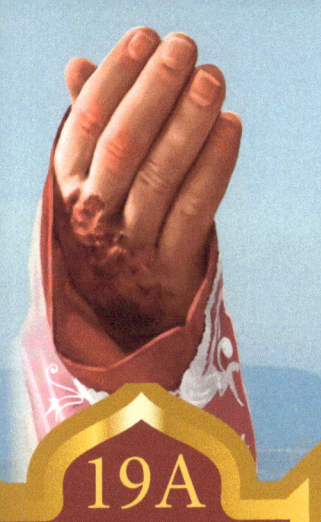

19A

I Love You, Pio

My children of Love, listen to me well.

Daily life on Earth is filled with the unexpected; it is characterized by ups and downs, frustration, and, in particular, inner imbalances of varying severities.

Dear hearts of my heart, I ask you to have prayer as your recourse as soon as possible in order to avoid drifting for too long. If faced with any misunderstandings, do not make enemies of those who try to be your friends.

Reach your hand out, be flexible, and reconcile with all the souls around you.

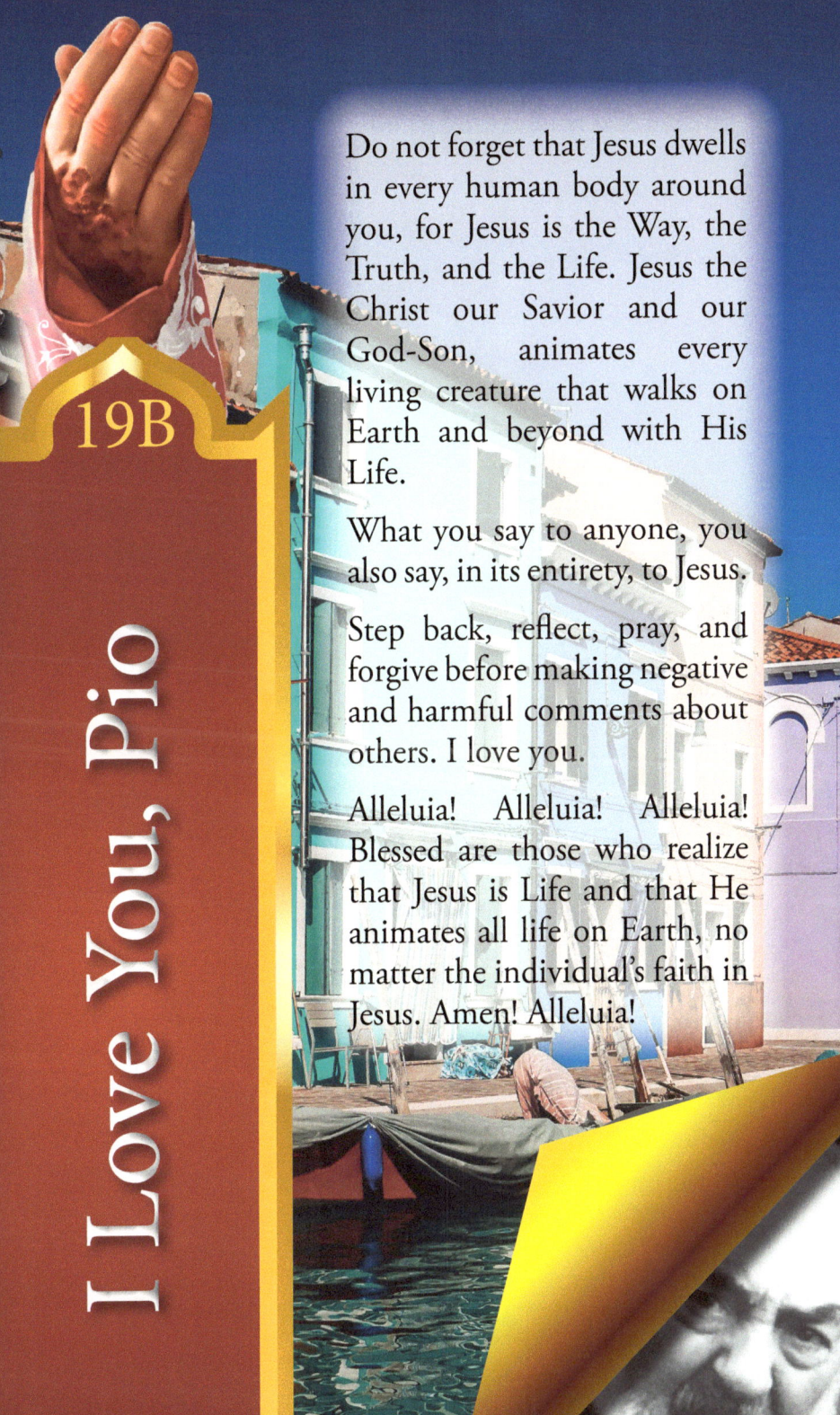

I Love You, Pio

19B

Do not forget that Jesus dwells in every human body around you, for Jesus is the Way, the Truth, and the Life. Jesus the Christ our Savior and our God-Son, animates every living creature that walks on Earth and beyond with His Life.

What you say to anyone, you also say, in its entirety, to Jesus.

Step back, reflect, pray, and forgive before making negative and harmful comments about others. I love you.

Alleluia! Alleluia! Alleluia! Blessed are those who realize that Jesus is Life and that He animates all life on Earth, no matter the individual's faith in Jesus. Amen! Alleluia!

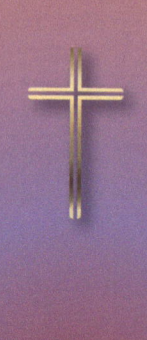

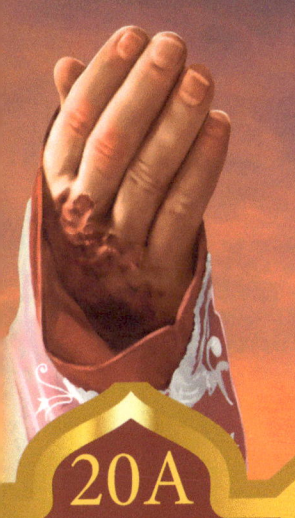

I Love You, Pio

20A

My friends, my tender hearts, listen to me carefully.

Unfortunately, fear is often present in your hearts. This fear, which invades you when you go through the trials of life, is well known to me, Saint Padre Pio, to all the Saints of Paradise, as well as to the Angels of God, Jesus, the Blessed Virgin Mary, and God the Father Almighty.

Satan can easily make you feel a false sense of loneliness marked by the abandonment of Heaven's inhabitants and the absence of or neglect from God, Jesus, and Mary.

To combat this, hasten to pray and clearly visualize my name,

20B

I Love You, Pio

my face, and my mission, and pray firmly! I run with joy, solicitude, power and, above all, love and I stand before you, my beloved, my child, my little soul on this lost Earth.

In an instant, the miraculous solution to the problems you encounter will be presented to you in your mind and your heart; from this point on, the expected miracle will materialize. I love you.

Alleluia! Alleluia! Alleluia! Blessed are those who pray immediately when fear overcomes them, for deliverance from this fear is guaranteed in the first second of prayer, as ordained by God. Amen! Alleluia!

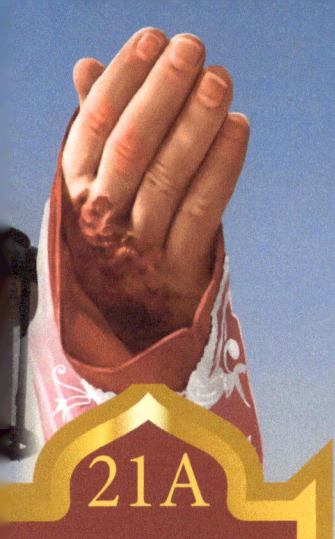

21A

I Love You, Pio

My loves, my hearts, listen to me carefully.

The events of the end are already here—I have already told you this, and I will repeat this unto you again. You may hear horrific news from around the world, such as news about terrorist crimes, natural disasters, global calamities, scandals, and unimaginable atrocities.

Verily, verily, I say unto you: The end times are here, and the global changes will be terrifying and shocking to the entire population, regardless of one's financial, social, professional, and personal position, or religion, whether

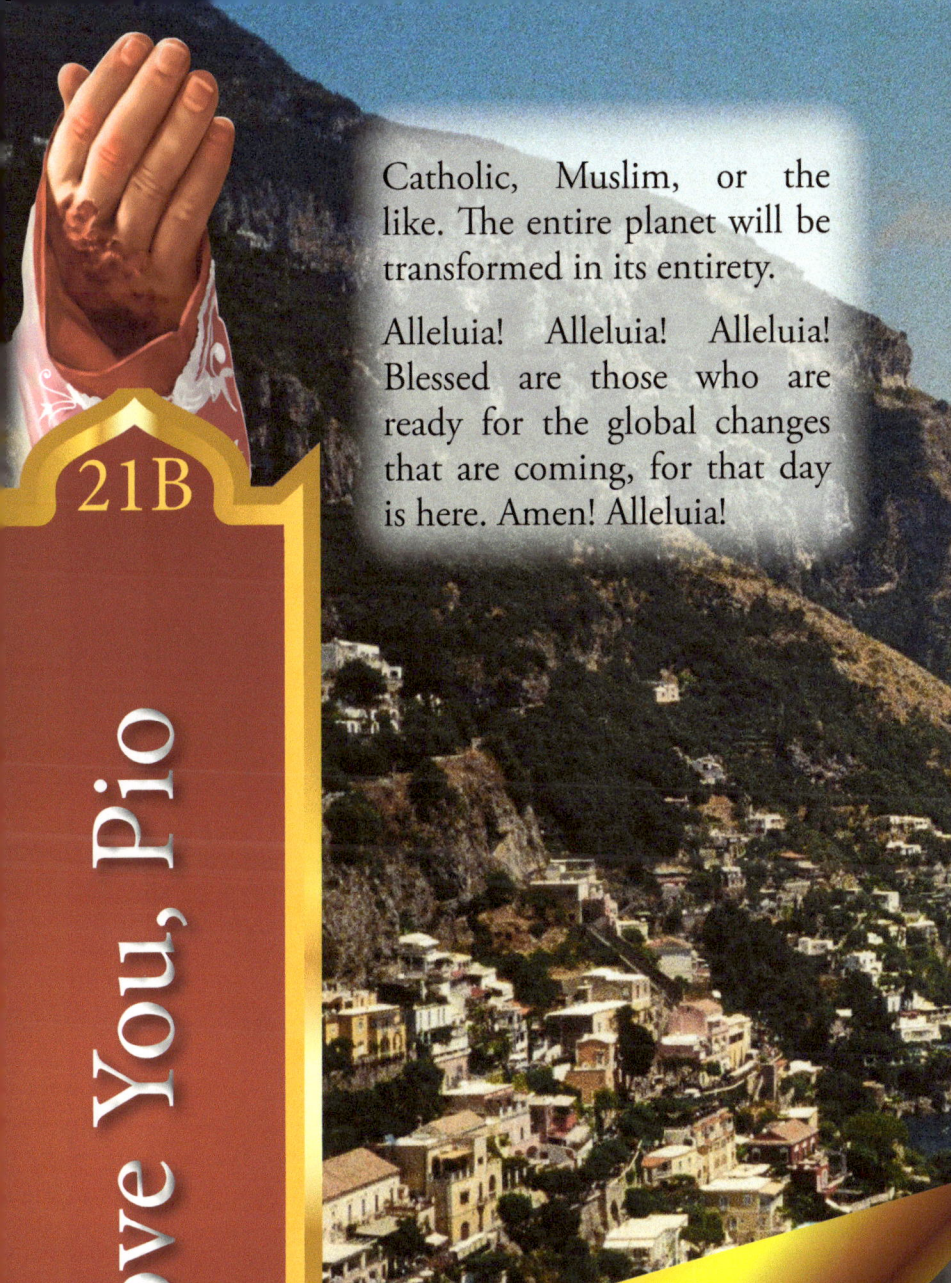

Catholic, Muslim, or the like. The entire planet will be transformed in its entirety.

Alleluia! Alleluia! Alleluia! Blessed are those who are ready for the global changes that are coming, for that day is here. Amen! Alleluia!

I Love You, Pio

21B

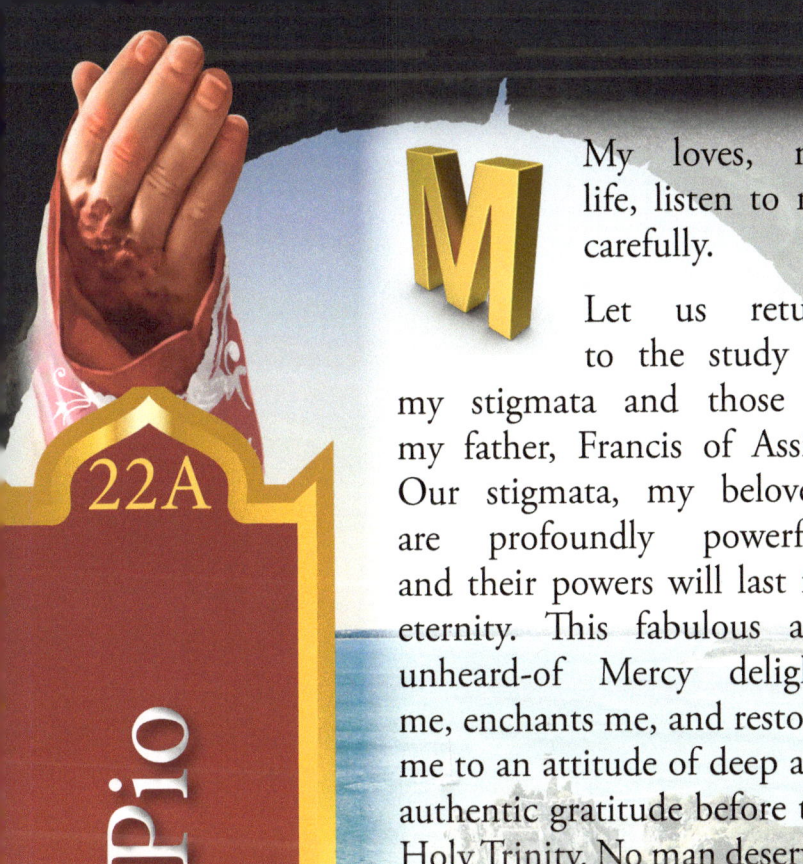

22A

I Love You, Pio

My loves, my life, listen to me carefully.

Let us return to the study of my stigmata and those of my father, Francis of Assisi. Our stigmata, my beloved, are profoundly powerful, and their powers will last for eternity. This fabulous and unheard-of Mercy delights me, enchants me, and restores me to an attitude of deep and authentic gratitude before the Holy Trinity. No man deserves so much generosity, greatness, abundance, and, above all, so much love. This is expressed here, imprinted in my flesh, and experienced in daily life by you, my dear children; this is the true and immeasurable

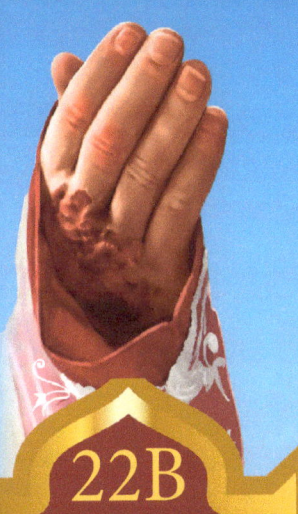

love of Abba Father.

Alleluia! Alleluia! Alleluia! Blessed are those who remain in a state of gratitude before the love manifested by Abba Father through my stigmata and those of my father Francis. Amen! Alleluia!

22B

I Love You, Pio

23

I Love You, Pio

My friends, my loves, my hearts, listen to me carefully. My visits to your side will become more frequent, last longer, and be more powerful; above all, they will be more beneficial for the salvation of your soul and your final entry into Paradise after the passage that is death. Our mystical union is real. Moreover, our magnetic attraction is blessed by God, and our intellectual and mutual understanding is in continuous development through your reading this series. Alleluia! Alleluia! Alleluia! Blessed are the chosen ones of my heart and the chosen ones of the stigmata, for Mercy and abundance are promised to them. Amen! Alleluia!

24 — I Love You, Pio

My friends, my loves, my hearts, and my joys, listen to me carefully.

We continue our studies of stigmata. The manifestation of the stigmata in my body represents a unique cosmic moment in the history of Creation. I would like to point out to you here that the manifestation of my stigmata is different from those of Father Francis. I will explain this to you very soon.

Alleluia! Alleluia! Alleluia! Blessed are those who study stigmata as well as those of Father Francis, for Mercy will be granted to them. Amen! Alleluia!

25A — I Love You, Pio

My friends, my loves, listen to me again.

The Seraphim Angel of Jesus, Abidranaël, appeared to me several times during my priesthood. He revealed to me the sweet message of the stigmata to come. On one miraculous day, Abidranaël approached me significantly, to the point of his etheric fusion with me—that is to say, his internal fusion with me on several levels and through multiple dimensions that you do not know.

His fusion with me elevated my soul to a level of ineffable, incredible, and above all, creative bliss. This is why my

25B

I Love You, Pio

stigmata appeared—vessels of eternal Grace, tunnels of infinite Divine Mercy, and above all abandonment to Jesus in all His Christic plenitude: the Body, Blood, Soul and Divinity of Jesus our Lord and our God.

Alleluia! Alleluia! Alleluia! Blessed are those who love Angels, for Angels will be their Divine protectors and their liaisons with God. Amen! Alleluia!

26A

I Love You, Pio

My loves, my hearts, my joy, listen to me carefully.

The anatomy of my stigmata is completely different than what you might have imagined. Indeed, there are no holes in them, unlike those of Father Francis. My stigmata were and remain transformations of the constituent tissues of my hand into a spongy and compressible consistency that resembles soft tissue.

It is impossible to see opening or holes in my stigmata. The tissues that form the basis of the stigmata are constantly soaked with blood—the blood of Jesus Christ, our

Savior. The base consists of reddish, granular tissue, much like red meat in a state of constant bleeding. The pain I experience is constant. I love you.

Alleluia! Alleluia! Alleluia! Blessed are the souls who pray to God through my stigmata and those of Father Francis. Amen! Alleluia!

26B

I Love You, Pio

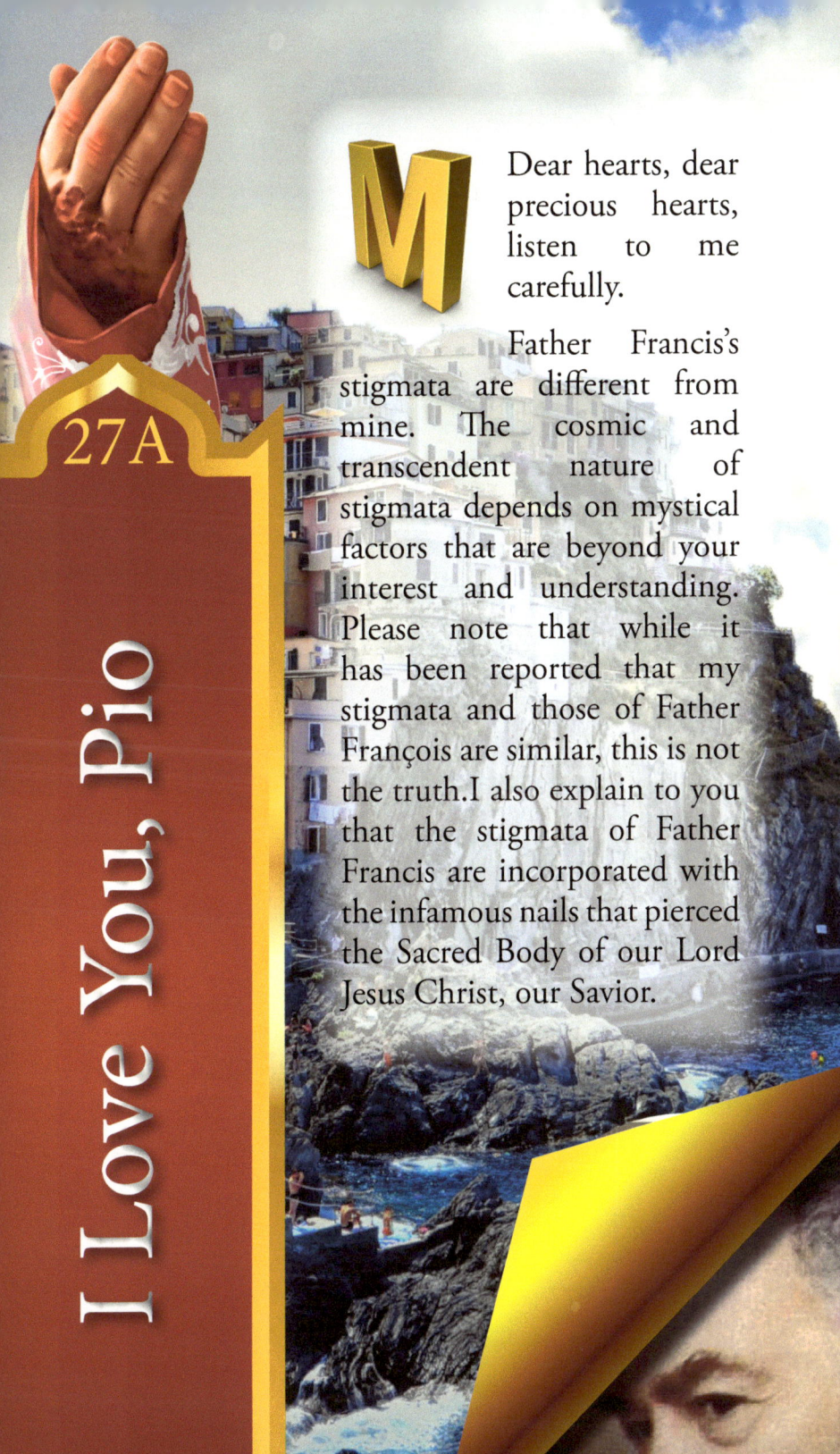

27A

I Love You, Pio

MDear hearts, dear precious hearts, listen to me carefully.

Father Francis's stigmata are different from mine. The cosmic and transcendent nature of stigmata depends on mystical factors that are beyond your interest and understanding. Please note that while it has been reported that my stigmata and those of Father François are similar, this is not the truth. I also explain to you that the stigmata of Father Francis are incorporated with the infamous nails that pierced the Sacred Body of our Lord Jesus Christ, our Savior.

The stigmata of Father Francis open the way to the total transformation of the soul and its complete conversion into an obedient and devoted disciple of God. I love you.

Alleluia! Alleluia! Alleluia! Blessed is he who prays with Saint Francis of Assisi, the Saint of total transformation. Amen! Alleluia!

27B

I Love You, Pio

28A

I Love You, Pio

MDear hearts, dear children, listen to me carefully.

My stigmata differ from those of Father Francis on several levels. Firstly, the stigmata of Father Francis are universal in nature—they have a global scope that spans the entire human scale. When an individual on Earth prays to God through the stigmata of Father Francis, the human population across the globe benefits.

My stigmata are different. Any soul who prays through my stigmata is elevated before Abba Father exclusively, directly, miraculously, and eternally. The applied theology,

the ineffable beatitude, the individual Divine Mercy, and the glory to God the Father as a result are unique to my stigmata, those of your servant, Saint Padre Pio, a humble priest of the friar minors. I love you.

28B

I Love You, Pio

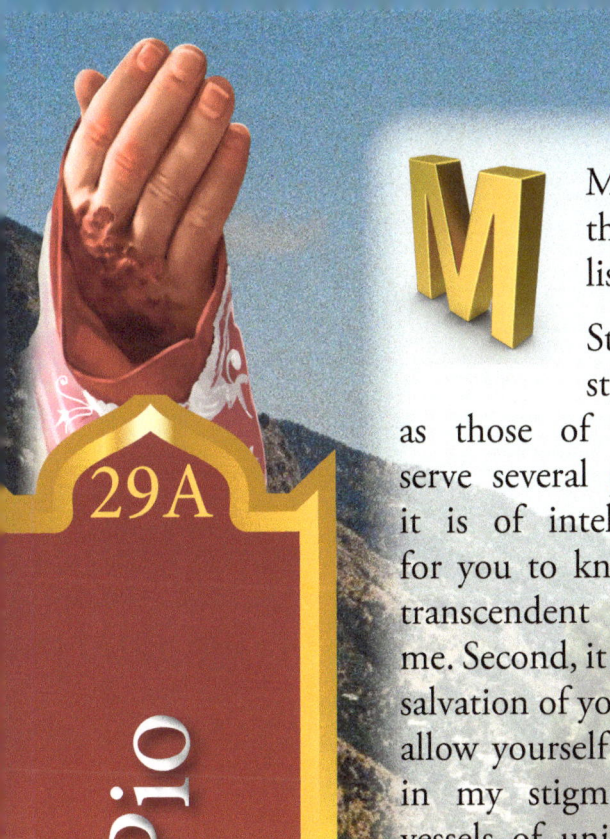

29A

I Love You, Pio

My children of the whole Earth, listen to me well.

Studies on my stigmata as well as those of Father Francis serve several purposes. First, it is of intellectual interest for you to know about these transcendent teachings from me. Second, it is critical for the salvation of your soul that you allow yourself to be absorbed in my stigmata, which are vessels of unique Grace that transport you directly into the Heart of Abba Father. Third, intimacy with me, Saint Padre Pio, a humble servant of the friar minors, is sweet and comfortable and will last for

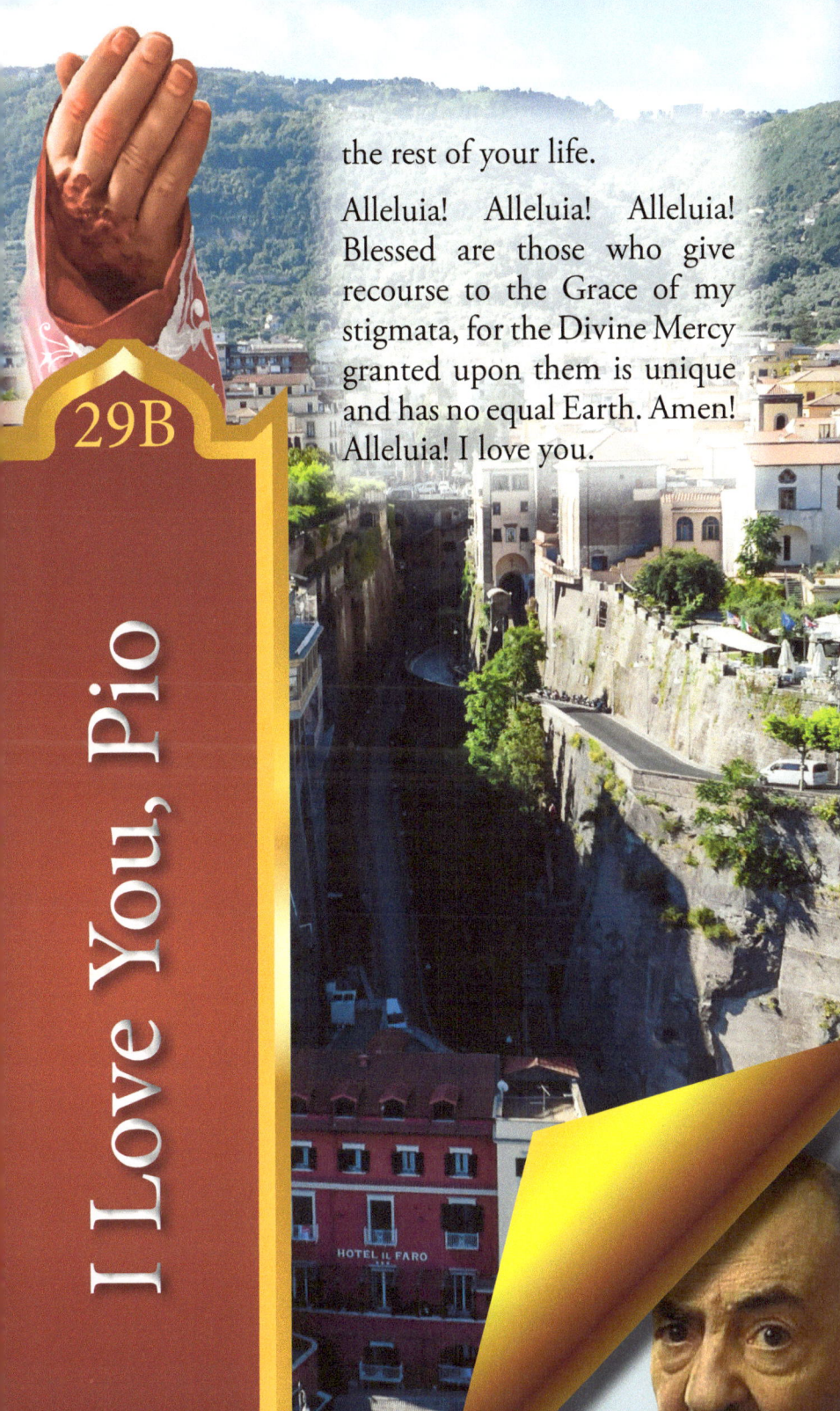

the rest of your life.

Alleluia! Alleluia! Alleluia! Blessed are those who give recourse to the Grace of my stigmata, for the Divine Mercy granted upon them is unique and has no equal Earth. Amen! Alleluia! I love you.

29B

I Love You, Pio

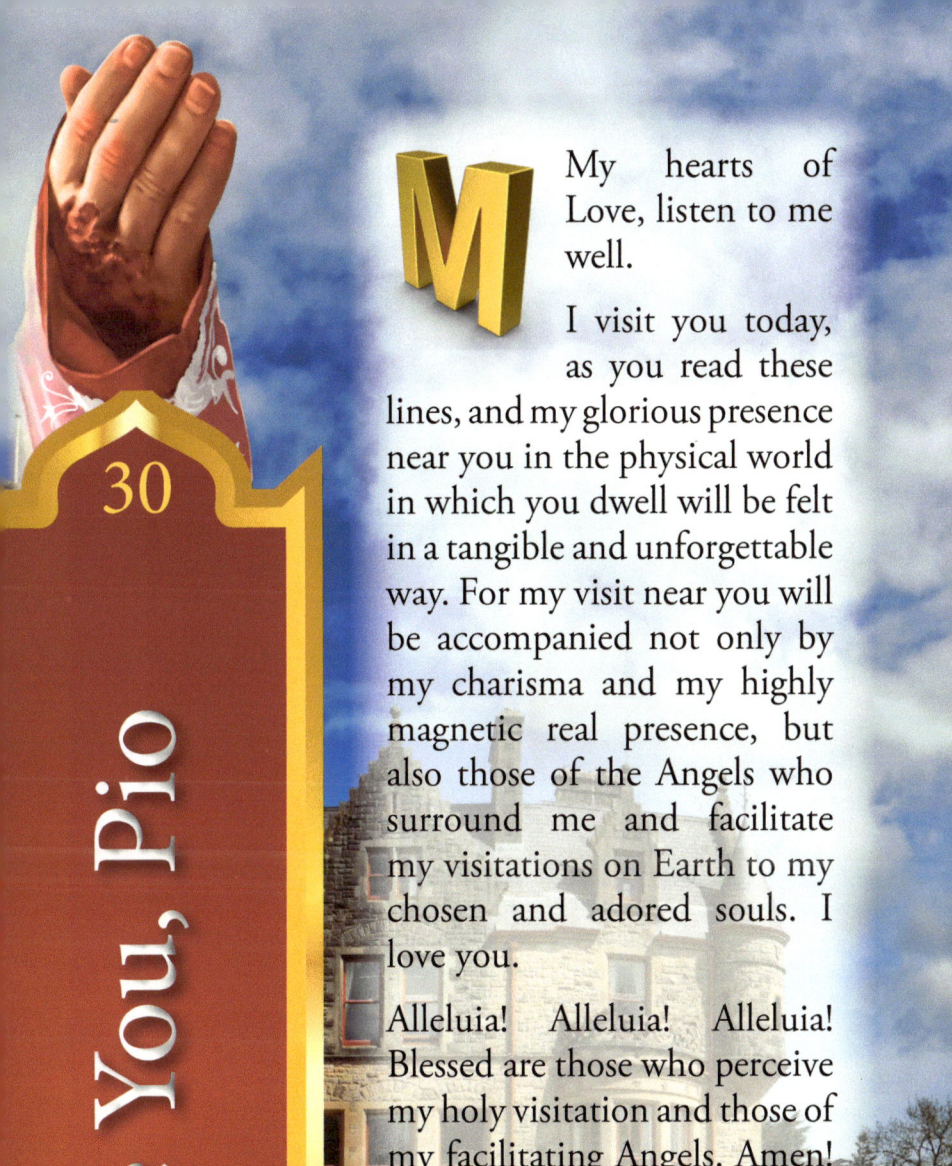

I Love You, Pio

30

My hearts of Love, listen to me well.

I visit you today, as you read these lines, and my glorious presence near you in the physical world in which you dwell will be felt in a tangible and unforgettable way. For my visit near you will be accompanied not only by my charisma and my highly magnetic real presence, but also those of the Angels who surround me and facilitate my visitations on Earth to my chosen and adored souls. I love you.

Alleluia! Alleluia! Alleluia! Blessed are those who perceive my holy visitation and those of my facilitating Angels. Amen! Alleluia! I love you.

My hearts, my joy, my children, listen to me well.

There is life in Paradise that awaits you beyond this transcendent teaching, for the Divine Mercy present in the stigmata includes a unique blessing: your glorious entrance into Paradise after the passage that is death.

Alleluia! Alleluia! Alleluia! Blessed are those who trust in my stigmata, for their life in Paradise has already begun through their faith in me. Amen! Alleluia!

I Love You, Pio

I Love You, Pio

32A

My Hearts of my heart, listen to me well.

The gift eternal life, which is promised and presented to you, is great. The privilege of the stigmata contains much more than the blessing of the Gates of Paradise, which will open wide after the passage that is death. My stigmata represent and allow the ineffable beatitudes of Paradise under the charm and sweetness of the Virgin Mary, your Divine Mother and my most benevolent Mother. I love you.

Alleluia! Alleluia! Alleluia! Blessed are those who access Paradise through my stigmata,

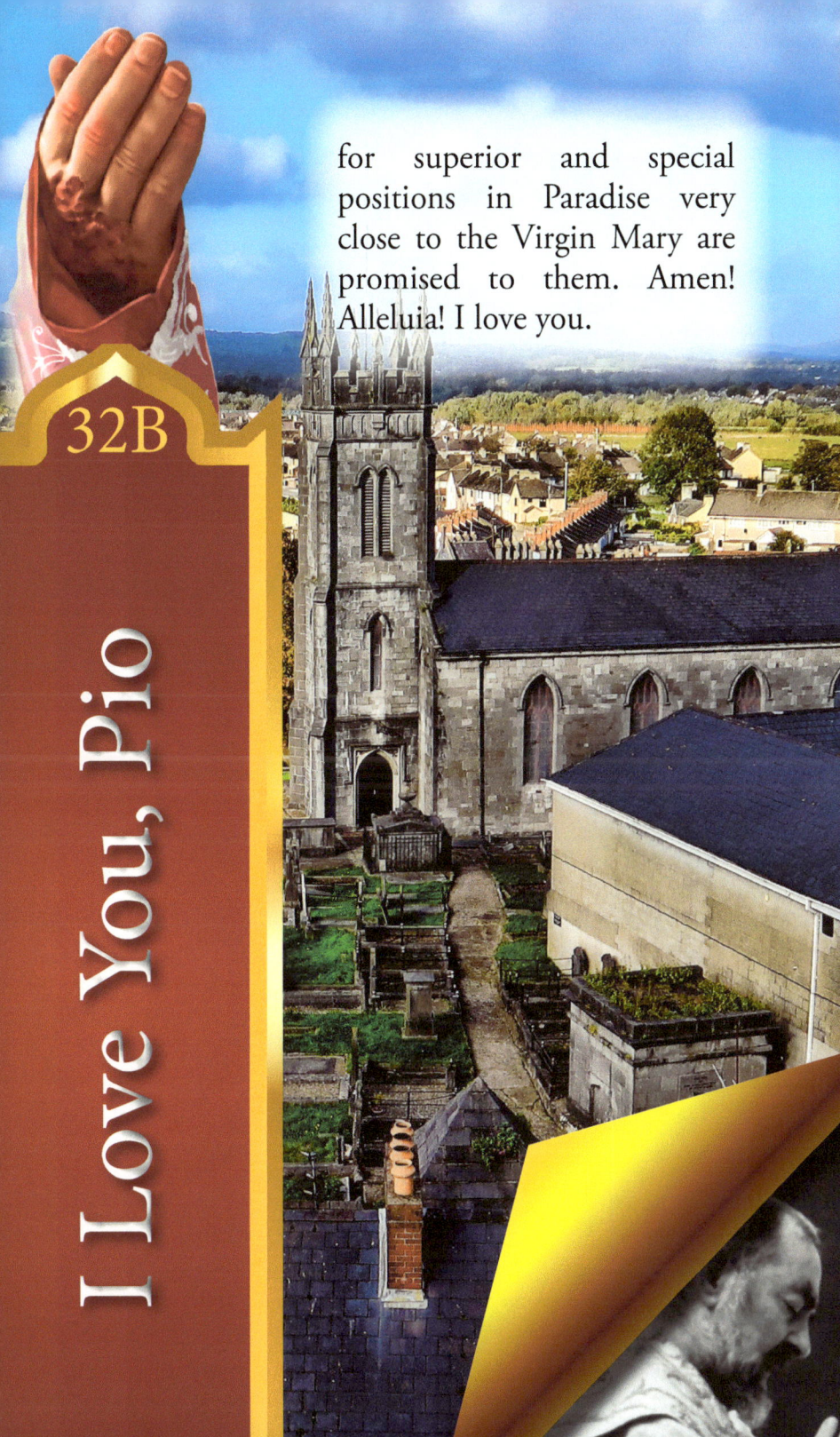

for superior and special positions in Paradise very close to the Virgin Mary are promised to them. Amen! Alleluia! I love you.

32B

I Love You, Pio

I Love You, Pio

My children, my hearts, my life on Earth, listen to me carefully.

I am coming to the end of this presentation about my stigmata and those of Father Francis. In addition, I am preparing another book that will enlighten you with Grace and Love.

Recite your rosary every day with the Virgin Mary, our Sweet Mother, and call upon me as a companion as you recite the rosary, a confessor, and, above all, miraculous intercessor in the Heart of Abba Father, for my stigmata have no equal on Earth by the Grace of Jesus our Lord and our God, Grace Incarnate, Divine Mercy made flesh.

I love you.

Pio.

My hearts, my joys, listen to me well. Your life will forever be miraculously transformed after reading this book. Only on the Day of Judgment will you appreciate the gift of Heaven that is given to you here.

Glory to the Father in the highest Heavens, and peace on Earth to men of good will.

The Virgin Mary, Your Divine Mother

SAN GIOVANNI ROTONDO, ITALY - APRIL 2, 2022: Interior of sanctuary of Saint Pio of Pietrelcina (Padre Pio Church) in San Giovanni Rotondo

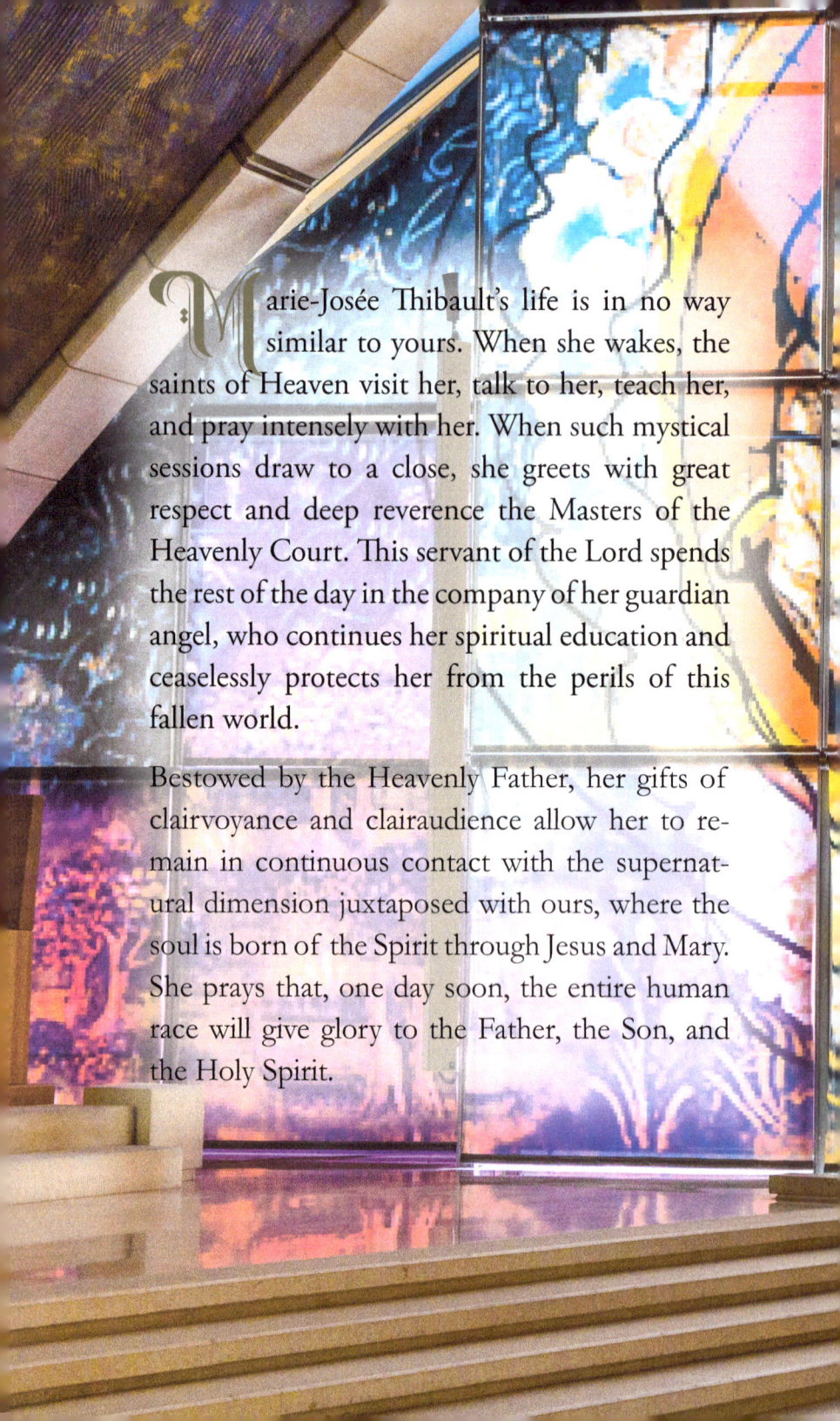

Marie-Josée Thibault's life is in no way similar to yours. When she wakes, the saints of Heaven visit her, talk to her, teach her, and pray intensely with her. When such mystical sessions draw to a close, she greets with great respect and deep reverence the Masters of the Heavenly Court. This servant of the Lord spends the rest of the day in the company of her guardian angel, who continues her spiritual education and ceaselessly protects her from the perils of this fallen world.

Bestowed by the Heavenly Father, her gifts of clairvoyance and clairaudience allow her to remain in continuous contact with the supernatural dimension juxtaposed with ours, where the soul is born of the Spirit through Jesus and Mary. She prays that, one day soon, the entire human race will give glory to the Father, the Son, and the Holy Spirit.

San Giovanni Rotondo, 01 June 2017. Internal view of Sanctuary of San Giovanni Rotondo, in Apulia, region, south Italy.

- Abba, Your Father, Speaks: Book I
- Abba, Your Father, Speaks: Book II
- Abba, Your Father, Speaks: Book III
- Abba, Your Father, Speaks: Book IV
- Dear Humanity: Book 1
- Dear Humanity: Book 2
- St Therese of Lisieux Speaks - Book 1: I Am The Heart of the Rose
- Saint Francis of Assisi Speaks - Book 1
- Saint Francis of Assisi Speaks - Book 2
- Saint Martin de Porres Speaks - Book 1
- Saint Bernadette Speaks - Book 1
- Saint Joan of Arc Speaks - Book 1
- Saint Padre Pio Speaks: Book 1
- Saint Beethoven Speaks - Book 1
- Saint Barnabas Speaks - Book 1

Also by the Author

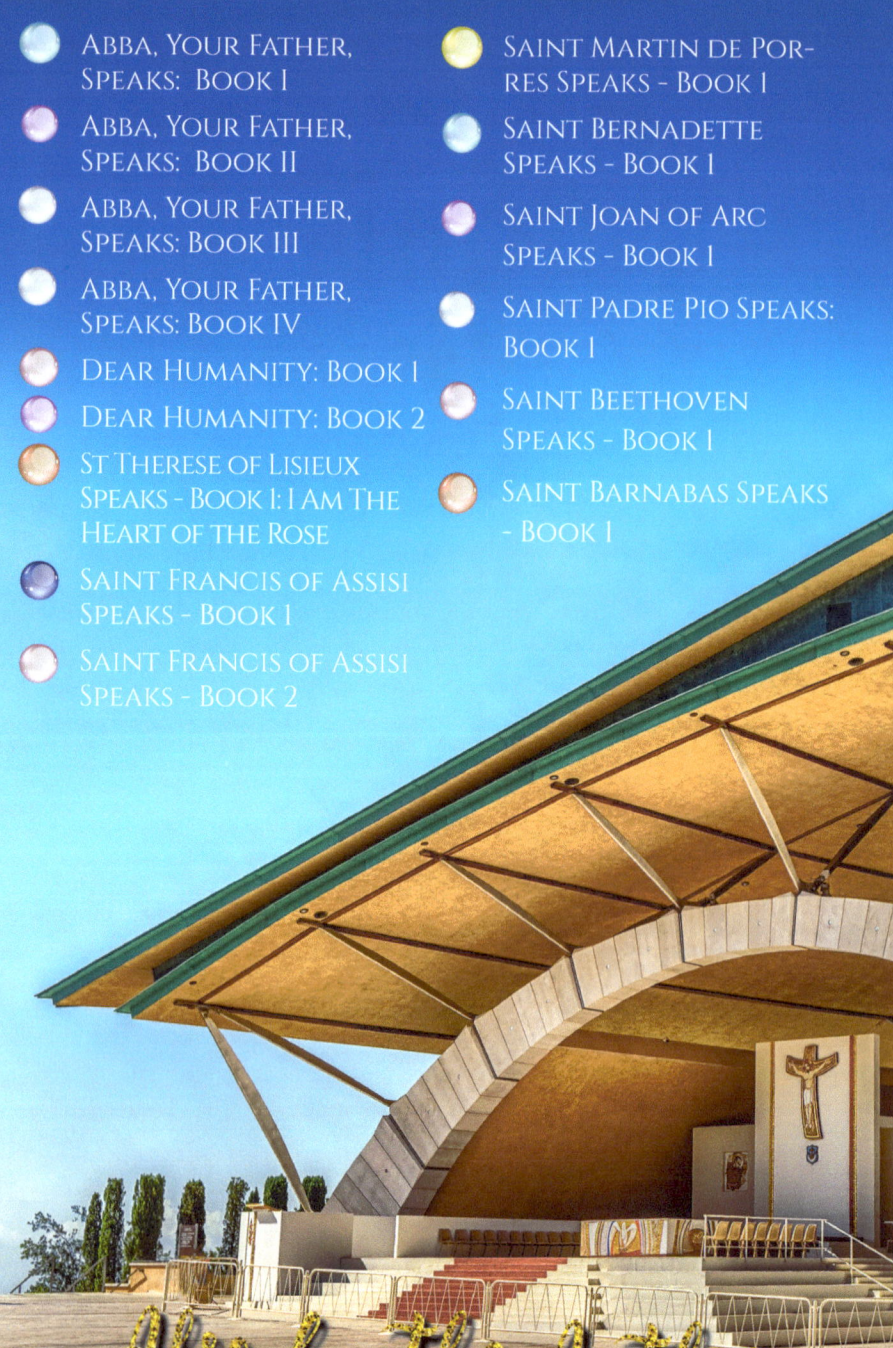

- Angel Gabriel Speaks: Book 1
- The Holy Pope Saint John Paul II Speaks - Book 1
- The Holy Pope Saint John Paul II Speaks - Book 2
- Prophet Moses Speaks 1
- Saint John the Baptist Speaks

Exterior view of Church of Saint Mary of the Graces, in the Shrine of Saint Father Pious from Pietralcina in San Giovanni Rotondo, in Apulia in Italy

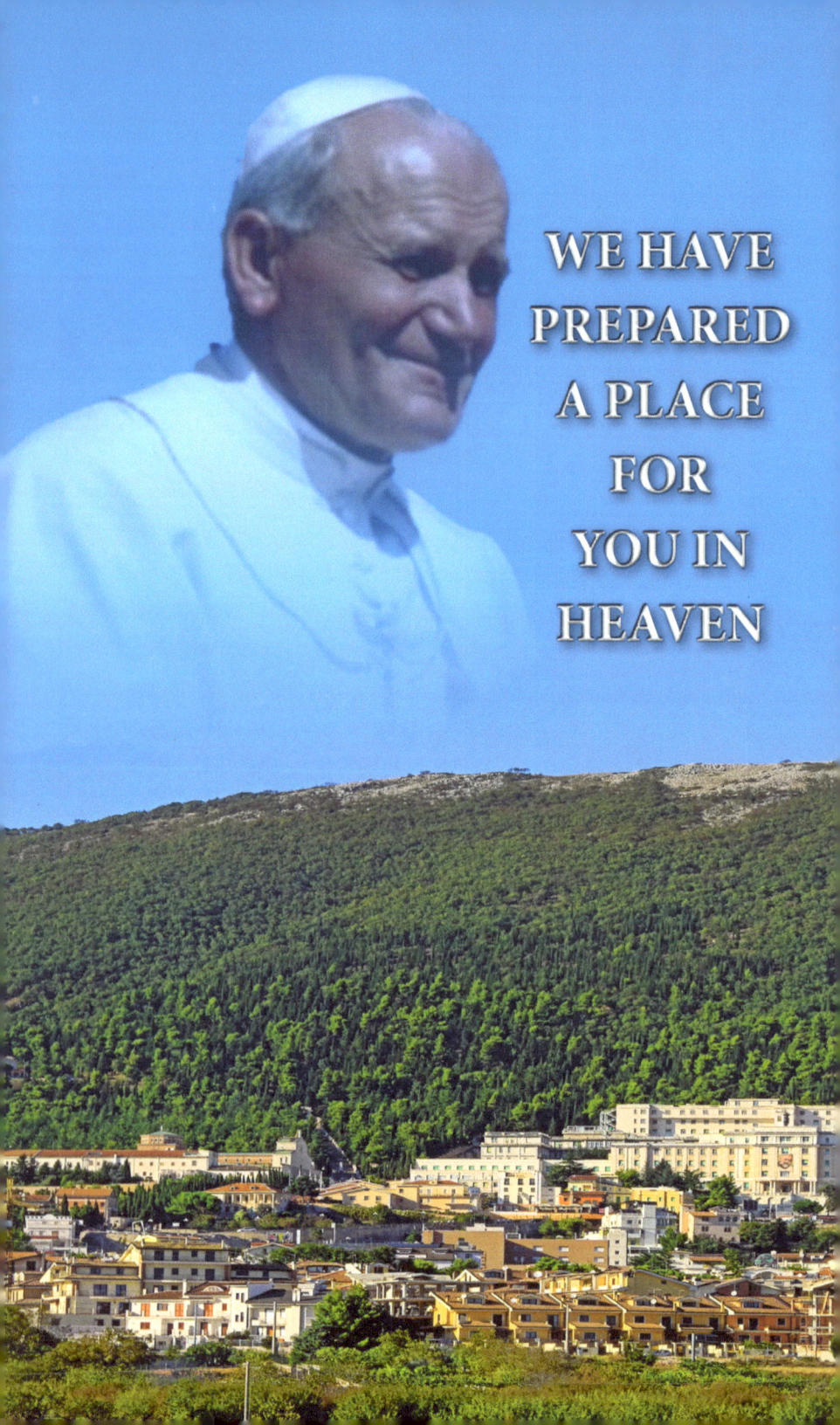

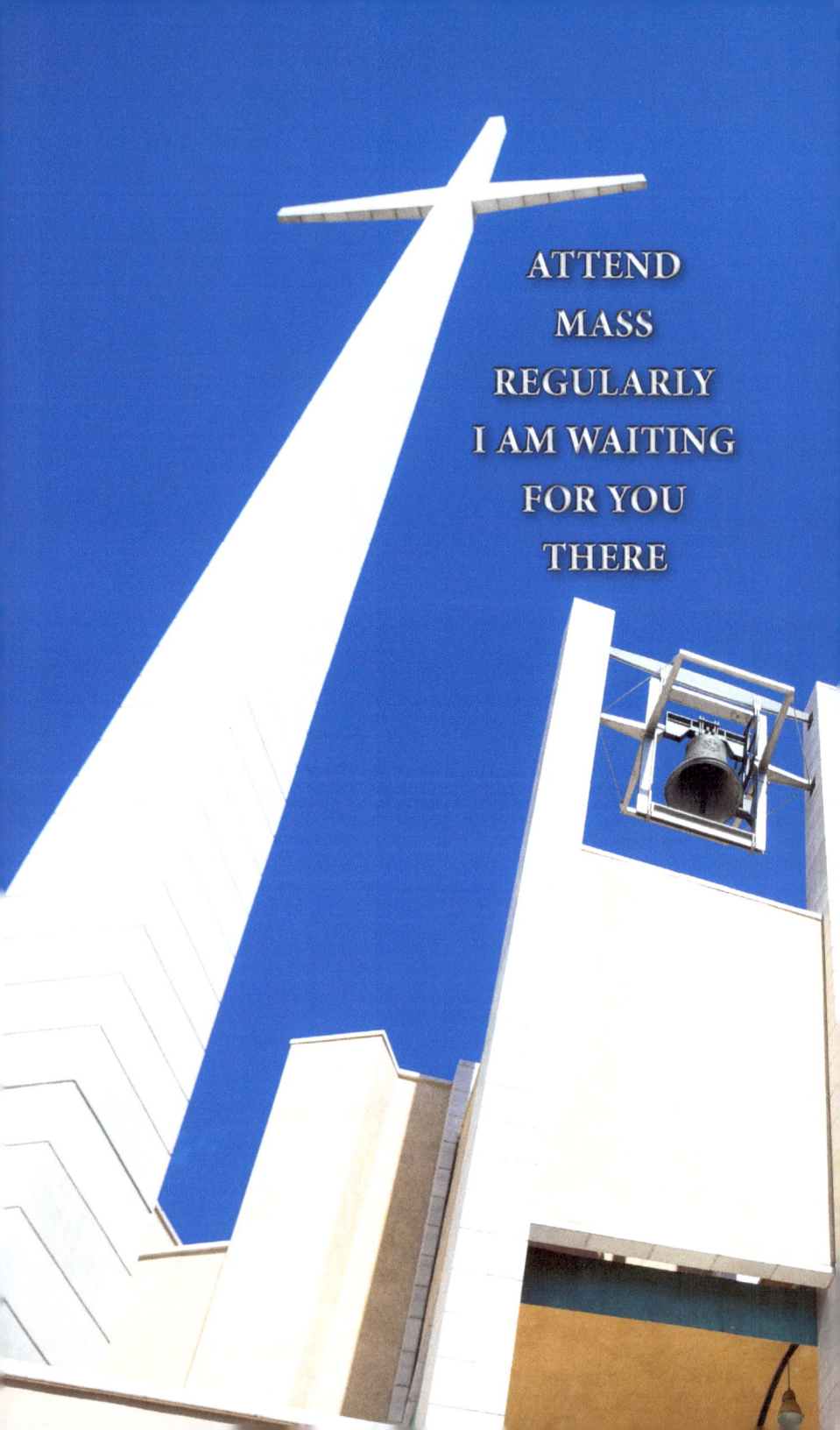